The Constitution of
The State of Indiana:
A Quick Reference Guide

Bootblack Budget Books
Copyright 2018 ©
ISBN-13: 978-1986106542
ISBN-10: 1986106543

Contents:

Preamble – Page 24

Article I: Bill of Rights – Page 25

Section 1. Inherent Rights

Section 2. Right to Worship

Section 3. Freedom of Religious Opinions

Section 4. Freedom of Religion

Section 5. No Religious Test for Office

Section 6. No State Money for Religious Institutions

Section 7. Religion No Bar to Competency of Witnesses

Section 8. Mode of Oath Administration

Section 9. Freedom of Thought and Speech

Section 10. Libel, Truth as Defense

Section 11. Search and Seizure

Section 12. Openness of The Courts, Speedy Trial

Section 13. Rights of Accused, Rights of Victims

Section 14. Double Jeopardy and Self-Incrimination

Section 15. Rights of Persons Arrested

Section 16. Excessive Bail or Fines, Cruel and Unusual Punishment

Section 17. Bailable Offenses

Section 18. Penal Code and Reformation

Section 19. Criminal Cases--Jury Determination

Section 20. Civil Cases--Right of Trial by Jury

Section 21. Compensation for Services and Property

Section 22. Debts--Imprisonment Exemption

Section 23. Equal Privileges and Immunities

Section 24. Ex Post Facto Laws

Section 25. Laws--Taking Effect

Section 26. Suspension of Laws

Section 27. Habeas Corpus

Section 28. Treason Defined

Section 29. Treason, Proof

Section 30. Effect of Conviction

Section 31. Right of Assemblage And Petition

Section 32. Arms--Right to Bear

Section 33. Military

Section 34. Quartering of soldiers

Section 35. Titles of Nobility

Section 36. Freedom of Emigration

Section 37. Slavery--Prohibition

Section 38. The Right to Hunt, Fish, and Harvest Wildlife

Article II: Suffrage and Election – Page 32

Section 1. Elections

Section 2. Voting Qualifications

Section 3. Repealed

Section 4. State Residence

Section 5. Repealed

Section 6. Bribery

Section 7. Repealed

Section 8. Disfranchisement for Infamous Crime

Section 9. Lucrative Offices--Eligibility

Section 10. Accountability of Defaulters

Section 11. Pro Tempore Appointments

Section 12. Freedom from Arrest

Section 13. Election Methods

Section 14. Time of Elections--Registration

Article III: Distribution of Powers – Page 35

Section 1. Three Departments

Article IV: Legislative – Page 36

Section 1. General Assembly

Section 2. Number of Members

Section 3. Term of Office

Section 4. Vacancies

Section 5. Apportionment

Section 6. Repealed

Section 7. Qualifications

Section 8. Privileges

Section 9. Sessions

Section 10. Organization and Procedure

Section 11. Quorum

Section 12. Journals

Section 13. Public Sessions

Section 14. Discipline of Members

Section 15. Contempt

Section 16. General Powers

Section 17. Origin of bills

Section 18. Reading of Bills

Section 19. Subject-Matter of Bills

Section 20. Wording

Section 21. Repealed

Section 22. Local and Special Laws

Section 23. Generality of Laws

Section 24. Suits Against the State

Section 25. Passage of Bills

Section 26. Protests

Section 27. Public Laws

Section 28. Date Acts take Effect

Section 29. Compensation

Section 30. Eligibility for Office

Article V: Executive – Page 43

Section 1. Governor

Section 2. Lieutenant governor

Section 3. Election

Section 4. Vote

Section 5. Tie Vote

Section 6. Contesting the Election

Section 7. Eligibility

Section 8. Ineligibility

Section 9. Term of Office

Section 10. Vacancies

Section 11. President of the Senate

Section 12. Commander-in-Chief

Section 13. Recommendations

Section 14. Action on Bills

Section 15. Transaction of Business

Section 16. Execution of Laws

Section 17. Reprieves--Commutations--Pardons

Section 18. Vacancies in Office

Section 19. Repealed

Section 20. Meeting Place of General Assembly

Section 21. Rights and Duties of Lieutenant Governor

Section 22. Compensation of Governor

Section 23. Compensation of Lieutenant Governor

Section 24. Ineligible for other Office

Article VI: Administrative – Page 52

Section 1. State Officers

Section 2. County Officers

Section 3. Statutory Officers

Section 4. Qualifications of County Officers

Section 5. Residence of State Officers

Section 6. Residence of Other Officers

Section 7. Impeachment of State Officers

Section 8. Impeachment of Other Officers

Section 9. Vacancies

Section 10. County Boards

Section 11. Repealed

Article VII: Judicial – Page 55

Section 1. Judicial Power

Section 2. Supreme Court

Section 3. Chief Justice

Section 4. Jurisdiction of Supreme Court

Section 5. Court of Appeals

Section 6. Jurisdiction of Court of Appeals

Section 7. Judicial Circuits

Section 8. Circuit Courts

Section 9. Judicial Nominating Commission

Section 10. Selection of Justices of the Supreme Court and Judges of the Court of Appeals

Section 11. Tenure of Justices of Supreme Court and Judges of the Court of Appeals

Section 12. Substitution of Judges

Section 13. Removal of Circuit Court Judges and Prosecuting Attorneys

Section 14. Repealed

Section 15. No Limitation on Term of Office

Section 16. Prosecuting Attorneys

Section 17. Grand Jury

Section 18. Criminal Prosecutions

Section 19. Pay

Section 20. Repealed

Section 21. Repealed

Article VIII: Education – Page 62

Section 1. Common School System

Section 2. Common School Fund

Section 3. Principal and Income

Section 4. Investment and Distribution

Section 5. Reinvestment

Section 6. Liability of Counties

Section 7. Trust Funds

Section 8. Superintendent of Public Instruction

Article IX: State Institutions – Page 65

Section 1. Deaf, Mute, Blind, and the Insane

Section 2. Juvenile Offenders

Section 3. County Farms

Article X: Finance – Page 66

Section 1. Assessment and Taxation

Section 2. Disposition of Revenue

Section 3. Appropriations

Section 4. Publication of Statement

Section 5. State Debt

Section 6. Counties

Section 7. Wabash and Erie Canal

Section 8. Income Tax

Article XI: Corporations – Page 71

Section 1. Banks

Section 2. Laws

Section 3. Money

Section 4. Branches

Section 5. Responsibility of Branches

Section 6. Repealed

Section 7. Redemption

Section 8. Preference

Section 9. Interest

Section 10. Repealed

Section 11. Trust Funds

Section 12. State as Stockholder

Section 13. Other Corporations Formation

Section 14. Liability

Article XII: Militia – Page 74

Section 1. Composition

Section 2. Commander-in-Chief

Section 3. Adjutant General

Section 4. Conscientious Objectors

Section 5. Repealed

Section 6. Repealed

Article XIII: Political and Municipal Corporations – Page 75

Section 1. Debt Limitation

Section 2. Repealed

Section 3. Repealed

Section 4. Repealed

Article XIV: Boundaries – Page 76

Section 1. State

Section 2. Jurisdiction and Sovereignty

Article XV: Miscellaneous – Page 77

Section 1. Selection of Officers

Section 2. Duration of Office

Section 3. Extension of Office

Section 4. Oath

Section 5. State Seal

Section 6. Commissions

Section 7. County Areas

Section 8. Repealed

Section 9. State Grounds

Section 10. Tippecanoe Battle Ground

Article XVI: Amendments – Page 79

Section 1. Amendments

Section 2. Submission

23

Schedule – Page 80

Preamble

TO THE END, that justice be established, public order maintained, and liberty perpetuated; WE, the People of the State of Indiana, grateful to ALMIGHTY GOD for the free exercise of the right to choose our own form of government, do ordain this Constitution.

ARTICLE I: BILL OF RIGHTS

Section 1. Inherent Rights

WE DECLARE, That all people are created equal; that they are endowed by their CREATOR with certain inalienable rights; that among these are life, liberty, and the pursuit of happiness; that all power is inherent in the people; and that all free governments are, and of right ought to be, founded on their authority, and instituted for their peace, safety, and well-being. For the advancement of these ends, the people have, at all times, an indefeasible right to alter and reform their government.

Section 2. Right to Worship

All people shall be secured in the natural right to worship ALMIGHTY GOD, according to the dictates of their own consciences.

Section 3. Freedom of Religious Opinions

No law shall, in any case whatever, control the free exercise and enjoyment of religious opinions, or interfere with the rights of conscience.

Section 4. Freedom of Religion

No preference shall be given, by law, to any creed, religious society, or mode of worship; and no person shall be compelled to attend, erect, or support, any place of worship, or to maintain any ministry, against his consent.

Section 5. No Religious Test for Office

No religious test shall be required, as a qualification for any office of trust or profit.

Section 6. No State Money for Religious Institutions

No money shall be drawn from the treasury, for the benefit of any religious or theological institution.

Section 7. Religion No Bar to Competency of Witnesses

No person shall be rendered incompetent as a witness, in consequence of his opinions on matters of religion.

Section 8. Mode of Oath Administration

The mode of administering an oath or affirmation, shall be such as may be most consistent with, and binding upon, the conscience of the person, to whom such oath or affirmation may be administered.

Section 9. Freedom of Thought and Speech

No law shall be passed, restraining the free interchange of thought and opinion, or restricting the right to speak, write, or print, freely, on any subject whatever: but for the abuse of that right, every person shall be responsible.

Section 10. Libel, Truth as Defense

In all prosecutions for libel, the truth of the matters alleged to be libelous, may be given in justification.

Section 11. Search and Seizure

The right of the people to be secure in their persons, houses, papers, and effects, against unreasonable search or seizure, shall not be violated; and no warrant shall issue, but upon probable cause, supported by oath or affirmation, and particularly describing the place to be searched, and the person or thing to be seized.

Section 12. Openness of the Courts, Speedy Trial

All courts shall be open; and every person, for injury done to him in his person, property, or reputation, shall have remedy by due course of law. Justice shall be administered freely, and without purchase; completely, and without denial; speedily, and without delay.

Section 13. Rights of Accused, Rights of Victims

(a) In all criminal prosecutions, the accused shall have the right to a public trial, by an impartial jury, in the county in which the offense shall have been committed; to be heard by himself and counsel; to demand the nature and cause of the accusation against him, and to have a copy thereof; to meet the witnesses face to face, and to have compulsory process for obtaining witnesses in his favor.

(b) Victims of crime, as defined by law, shall have the right to be treated with fairness, dignity, and respect throughout the criminal justice process; and, as defined by law, to be informed of and present during public hearings and to confer with the prosecution, to the extent that exercising these rights does not infringe upon the constitutional rights of the accused.

Section 14. Double Jeopardy and Self-incrimination

No person shall be put in jeopardy twice for the same offense. No person, in any criminal prosecution, shall be compelled to testify against himself.

Section 15. Rights of Persons Arrested

No person arrested, or confined in jail, shall be treated with unnecessary rigor.

Section 16. Excessive Bail or Fines, Cruel and Unusual Punishment

Excessive bail shall not be required. Excessive fines shall not be imposed. Cruel and unusual punishments shall not be inflicted. All penalties shall be proportioned to the nature of the offense.

Section 17. Bailable Offenses

Offenses, other than murder or treason, shall be bailable by sufficient sureties. Murder or treason shall not be bailable, when the proof is evident, or the presumption strong.

Section 18. Penal Code and Reformation

The penal code shall be founded on the principles of reformation, and not of vindictive justice.

Section 19. Criminal Cases--Jury Determination

In all criminal cases whatever, the jury shall have the right to determine the law and the facts.

Section 20. Civil Cases--Right of Trial by Jury

In all civil cases, the right of trial by jury shall remain inviolate.

Section 21. Compensation for Services and Property

No person's particular services shall be demanded, without just compensation. No person's property shall be taken by law, without just compensation; nor, except in case of the State, without such compensation first assessed and tendered.

Section 22. Debts--Imprisonment Exemption:

The privilege of the debtor to enjoy the necessary comforts of life, shall be recognized by wholesome laws, exempting a reasonable amount of property from seizure or sale, for the payment of any debt or liability hereafter contracted: and there shall be no imprisonment for debt, except in case of fraud.

Section 23. Equal Privileges and Immunities

The General Assembly shall not grant to any citizen, or class of citizens, privileges or immunities, which, upon the same terms, shall not equally belong to all citizens.

Section 24. Ex Post Facto Laws

No ex post facto law, or law impairing the obligation of contracts, shall ever be passed.

Section 25. Laws--Taking Effect

No law shall be passed, the taking effect of which shall be made to depend upon any authority, except as provided in this Constitution.

Section 26. Suspension of Laws

The operation of the laws shall never be suspended, except by the authority of the General Assembly.

Section 27. Habeas Corpus

The privilege of the writ of habeas corpus shall not be suspended, except in case of rebellion or invasion; and then, only if the public safety demand it.

Section 28. Treason Defined

Treason against the State shall consist only in levying war against it, and in giving aid and comfort to its enemies.

Section 29. Treason, Proof

No person shall be convicted of treason, except on the testimony of two witnesses to the same overt act, or upon his confession in open court.

Section 30. Effect of Conviction

No conviction shall work corruption of blood, or forfeiture of estate.

Section 31. Right of Assemblage and Petition

No law shall restrain any of the inhabitants of the State from assembling together in a peaceable manner, to consult for their common good; nor from instructing their representatives; nor from applying to the General Assembly for redress of grievances.

Section 32. Arms--Right to Bear

The people shall have a right to bear arms, for the defense of themselves and the State.

Section 33. Military

The military shall be kept in strict subordination to the civil power.

Section 34. Quartering of Soldiers
No soldier shall, in time of peace, be quartered in any house, without the consent of the owner; nor, in time of war, but in a manner to be prescribed by law.

Section 35. Titles of Nobility

The General Assembly shall not grant any title of nobility, nor confer hereditary distinctions.

Section 36. Freedom of Emigration

Emigration from the State shall not be prohibited.

Section 37. Slavery—Prohibition

There shall be neither slavery, nor involuntary servitude, within the State, otherwise than for the punishment of crimes, whereof the party shall have been duly convicted.

Section 38. The Right to Hunt, Fish, and Harvest Wildlife

(a) The right to hunt, fish, and harvest wildlife:

(1) is a valued part of Indiana's heritage; and
(2) shall be forever preserved for the public good.

(b) The people have a right, which includes the right to use traditional methods, to hunt, fish, and harvest wildlife, subject only to the laws prescribed by the General Assembly and rules prescribed by virtue of the authority of the General Assembly to:

(1) promote wildlife conservation and management; and
(2) preserve the future of hunting and fishing.

(c) Hunting and fishing shall be a preferred means of managing and controlling wildlife.

(d) This section shall not be construed to limit the application of any provision of law relating to trespass or property rights.

ARTICLE II: SUFFRAGE AND ELECTIONS

Section 1. Elections

All elections shall be free and equal.

Section 2. Voting Qualifications

(a) A citizen of the United States who is at least eighteen (18) years of age and who has been a resident of a precinct thirty (30) days immediately preceding an election may vote in that precinct at the election.

(b) A citizen may not be disenfranchised under subsection (a), if the citizen is entitled to vote in a precinct under subsection (c) or federal law.

(c) The General Assembly may provide that a citizen who ceases to be a resident of a precinct before an election may vote in a precinct where the citizen previously resided if, on the date of the election, the citizen's name appears on the registration rolls for the precinct

Section 3. Repealed

Section 4. State Residence

No person shall be deemed to have lost his residence in the State, by reason of his absence, either on business of this State or of the United States.

Section 5. Repealed

Section 6. Bribery

Every person shall be disqualified from holding office, during the term for which he may have been elected, who shall have given or offered a bribe, threat, or reward, to procure his election.

Section 7. Repealed

Section 8. Disfranchisement for Infamous Crime

The General Assembly shall have power to deprive of the right of suffrage, and to render ineligible, any person convicted of an infamous crime.

Section 9. Lucrative Offices—Eligibility

No person holding a lucrative office or appointment under the United States or under this State is eligible to a seat in the General Assembly; and no person may hold more than one lucrative office at the same time, except as expressly permitted in this Constitution. Offices in the militia to which there is attached no annual salary shall not be deemed lucrative.

Section 10. Accountability of Defaulters

No person who may hereafter be a collector or holder of public moneys, shall be eligible to any office of trust or profit, until he shall have accounted for, and paid over, according to law, all sums for which he may be liable.

Section 11. Pro Tempore Appointments

In all cases in which it is provided, that an office shall not be filled by the same person more than a certain number of years continuously, an appointment pro tempore shall not be reckoned a part of that term.

Section 12. Freedom from Arrest

In all cases, except treason, felony, and breach of the peace, electors shall be free from arrest, in going to elections, during their attendance there, and in returning from the same.

Section 13. Election Methods

All elections by the People shall be by ballot; and all elections by the General Assembly, or by either branch thereof, shall be viva voce.

Section 14. Time of Elections—Registration

(a) General elections shall be held on the first Tuesday after the first Monday in November.

(b) The General Assembly may provide by law for the election of all judges of courts of general and appellate jurisdiction, by an election to be held for such officers only, at which time no other officer shall be voted for.

(c) The General Assembly shall provide for the registration of all persons entitled to vote.

ARTICLE III: DISTRIBUTION OF POWERS

Section 1. Three Departments

The powers of the Government are divided into three separate departments; the Legislative, the Executive including the Administrative, and the Judicial: and no person, charged with official duties under one of these departments, shall exercise any of the functions of another, except as in this Constitution expressly provided.

ARTICLE IV: LEGISLATIVE

Section 1. General Assembly

The Legislative authority of the State shall be vested in a General Assembly, which shall consist of a Senate and a House of Representatives. The style of every law shall be: "Be it enacted by the General Assembly of the State of Indiana;" and no law shall be enacted, except by bill.

Section 2. Number of Members

The Senate shall not exceed fifty, nor the House of Representatives one hundred members; and they shall be chosen by the electors of the respective districts into which the State may, from time to time, be divided.

Section 3. Term of Office

Senators shall be elected for the term of four years, and Representatives for the term of two years, from the day next after their general election. One half of the Senators, as nearly as possible, shall be elected biennially.

Section 4. Vacancies

The General Assembly may provide by law for the filling of such vacancies as may occur in the General Assembly.

Section 5. Apportionment

The General Assembly elected during the year in which a federal decennial census is taken shall fix by law the number of Senators and Representatives and apportion them among districts according to the number of inhabitants in each district, as revealed by that federal decennial census. The territory in each district shall be contiguous.

Section 6. Repealed

Section 7. Qualifications

No person shall be a Senator or a Representative, who, at the time of his election, is not a citizen of the United States; nor any one who has not been for two years next preceding his election, an inhabitant of this State, and, for one year next preceding his election, an inhabitant of the district whence he may be chosen. Senators shall be at least twenty-five, and Representatives at least twenty-one years of age.

Section 8. Privileges

Senators and Representatives, in all cases except treason, felony, and breach of the peace, shall be privileged from arrest, during the session of the General Assembly, and in going to and returning from the same; and shall not be subject to any civil process, during the session of the General Assembly, nor during the fifteen days next before the commencement thereof. For any speech or debate in either House, a member shall not be questioned in any other place.

Section 9. Sessions

The sessions of the General Assembly shall be held at the capitol of the State, commencing on the Tuesday next after the second Monday in January of each year in which the General Assembly meets unless a different day or place shall have been appointed by law. But if, in the opinion of the Governor, the public welfare shall require it, he may, at any time by proclamation, call a special session. The length and frequency of the sessions of the General Assembly shall be fixed by law.

Section 10. Organization and Procedure

Each House, when assembled, shall choose its own officers, the President of the Senate excepted; judge the elections, qualifications, and returns of its own members; determine its rules of proceeding, and sit upon its own adjournment. But neither House shall, without the consent of the other, adjourn for more than three days, nor to any place other than that in which it may be sitting.

Section 11. Quorum

Two-thirds of each House shall constitute a quorum to do business; but a smaller number may meet, adjourn from day to day, and compel the attendance of absent members. A quorum being in attendance, if either House fail to effect an organization within the first five days thereafter, the members of the House so failing, shall be entitled to no compensation, from the end of the said five days until an organization shall have been effected.

Section 12. Journals

Each House shall keep a journal of its proceedings, and publish the same. The yeas and nays, on any question, shall, at the request of any two members, be entered, together with the names of the members demanding the same, on the journal; Provided, that on a motion to adjourn, it shall require one-tenth of the members present to order the yeas and nays.

Section 13 Public Sessions

The doors of each House, and of Committees of the Whole, shall be kept open, except in such cases, as, in the opinion of either House, may require secrecy.

Section 14. Discipline of Members

Either House may punish its members for disorderly behavior, and may, with the concurrence of two-thirds, expel a member; but not a second time for the same cause.

Section 15. Contempt

Either House, during its session, may punish, by imprisonment, any person not a member, who shall have been guilty of disrespect to the House, by disorderly or contemptuous behavior, in its presence; but such imprisonment shall not, at any one time, exceed twenty-four hours.

Section 16. General Powers

Each House shall have all powers, necessary for a branch of the Legislative department of a free and independent State.

Section 17. Origin of Bills

Bills may originate in either House, but may be amended or rejected in the other; except that bills for raising revenue shall originate in the House of Representatives.

Section 18. Reading of Bills

Every bill shall be read, by title, on three several days, in each House; unless, in case of emergency, two-thirds of the House where such bill may be pending shall, by a vote of yeas and nays, deem it expedient to dispense with this rule; but the reading of a bill, by title, on its final passage, shall, in no case, be dispensed with; and the vote on the passage of every bill or joint resolution shall be taken by yeas and nays.

Section 19. Subject-Matter of Bills

An act, except an act for the codification, revision or rearrangement of laws, shall be confined to one subject and matters properly connected therewith.

Section 20. Wording

Every act and joint resolution shall be plainly worded, avoiding, as far as practicable, the use of technical terms.

Section 21 Repealed.

Section 22. Local and Special Laws

The General Assembly shall not pass local or special laws:

Providing for the punishment of crimes and misdemeanors;

Regulating the practice in courts of justice;

Providing for changing the venue in civil and criminal cases;

Granting divorces;

Changing the names of persons;

Providing for laying out, opening, and working on, highways, and for the election or appointment of supervisors;

Vacating roads, town plats, streets, alleys, and public squares;

Summoning and empaneling grand and petit juries, and providing for their compensation;

Regulating county and township business;
Regulating the election of county and township officers and their compensation;

Providing for the assessment and collection of taxes for State, county, township, or road purposes;

Providing for the support of common schools, or the preservation of school funds;

Relating to fees or salaries, except that the laws may be so made as to grade the compensation of officers in proportion to the population and the necessary services required;

Relating to interest on money;

Providing for opening and conducting elections of State, county, or township officers, and designating the places of voting;

Providing for the sale of real estate belonging to minors or other persons laboring under legal disabilities, by executors, administrators, guardians, or trustees.

Section 23. Generality of Laws

In all the cases enumerated in the preceding section, and in all other cases where a general law can be made applicable, all laws shall be general, and of uniform operation throughout the State.

Section 24. Suits Against the State

Provision may be made, by general law, for bringing suit against the State; but no special law authorizing such suit to be brought, or making compensation to any person claiming damages against the State, shall ever be passed.

Section 25. Passage of Bills

A majority of all the members elected to each House, shall be necessary to pass every bill or joint resolution; and all bills and joint resolutions so passed, shall be signed by the Presiding Officers of the respective Houses.

Section 26. Protests

Any member of either House shall have the right to protest, and to have his protest, with his reasons for dissent, entered on the journal.

Section 27. Public Laws

Every statute shall be a public law, unless otherwise declared in the statute itself.

Section 28. Date Acts Take Effect

No act shall take effect, until the same shall have been published and circulated in the several counties of the State, by authority, except in case of emergency, which emergency shall be declared in the preamble, or in the body, of the law.

Section 29. Compensation

The members of the General Assembly shall receive for their services a compensation to be fixed by law; but no increase of compensation shall take effect during the session at which such increase may be made.

Section 30. Eligibility for Office

No Senator or Representative shall, during the term for which he may have been elected, be eligible to any office, the election to which is vested in the General Assembly; nor shall he be appointed to any civil office of profit, which shall have been created, or the emoluments of which shall have been increased, during such term; but this latter provision shall not be construed to apply to any office elective by the People.

ARTICLE V: EXECUTIVE

Section 1. Governor

The executive power of the State shall be vested in a Governor. He shall hold his office during four years, and shall not be eligible more than eight years in any period of twelve years.

Section 2. Lieutenant Governor

There shall be a Lieutenant Governor, who shall hold his office during four years.

Section 3. Election

The Governor and Lieutenant Governor shall be elected at the times and places of choosing members of the General Assembly.

Section 4. Vote

Each candidate for Lieutenant Governor shall run jointly in the general election with a candidate for Governor, and his name shall appear jointly on the ballot with the candidate for Governor. Each vote cast for a candidate for Governor shall be considered cast for the candidate for Lieutenant Governor as well. The candidate for Lieutenant Governor whose name appears on the ballot jointly with that of the successful candidate for Governor shall be elected Lieutenant Governor.

Section 5. Tie Vote

In the event of a tie vote, the Governor and Lieutenant Governor shall be elected from the candidates having received the tie vote by the affirmative vote in joint session of a majority of the combined membership of both Houses as the first order of business after their organization.

Section 6. Contesting the Election

Contested elections for Governor or Lieutenant Governor, shall be determined by the General Assembly, in such manner as may be prescribed by law.

Section 7. Eligibility

No person shall be eligible to the office of Governor or Lieutenant Governor, who shall not have been five years a citizen of the United States, and also a resident of the State of Indiana during the five years next preceding his election; nor shall any person be eligible to either of the said offices, who shall not have attained the age of thirty years.

Section 8. Ineligibility

No member of Congress, or person holding any office under the United States or under this State, shall fill the office of Governor or Lieutenant Governor.

Section 9. Term of Office

The official term of the Governor and Lieutenant Governor shall commence on the second Monday of January, in the year one thousand eight hundred and fifty-three; and on the same day every fourth year thereafter.

Section 10. Vacancies

(a) In case the Governor-elect fails to assume office, or in case of the death or resignation of the Governor or the Governor's removal from office, the Lieutenant Governor shall become Governor and hold office for the unexpired term of the person whom the Lieutenant Governor succeeds. In case the Governor is unable to discharge the powers and duties of the office, the Lieutenant Governor shall discharge the powers and duties of the office as Acting Governor.

(b) Whenever there is a vacancy in the office of Lieutenant Governor, the Governor shall nominate a Lieutenant Governor who shall take office upon confirmation by a majority vote in each house of the General Assembly and hold office for the unexpired term of the previous Lieutenant Governor. If the General Assembly is not in session, the Governor shall call it into special session to receive and act upon the Governor's nomination. In the event of the inability of the Lieutenant Governor to discharge the powers and duties of the office, the General Assembly may provide by law for the manner in which a person shall be selected to act in the Lieutenant Governor's place and declare which powers and duties of the office such person shall discharge.

(c) Whenever the Governor transmits to the President pro tempore of the Senate and the Speaker of the House of Representatives the Governor's written declaration that the Governor is unable to discharge the powers and duties of the office, and until the Governor transmits to them a written declaration to the contrary, such powers and duties shall be discharged by the Lieutenant Governor as Acting Governor. Thereafter, when the Governor transmits to the President pro tempore of the Senate and the Speaker of the House of Representatives the Governor's written declaration that no inability exists, the Governor shall resume the powers and duties of the office.

(d) Whenever the President pro tempore of the Senate and the Speaker of the House of Representatives file with the Supreme Court a written statement suggesting that the Governor is unable to discharge the powers and duties of the office, the Supreme Court shall meet within forty-eight hours to decide the question and such decision shall be final. Thereafter, whenever the Governor files with the Supreme Court the Governor's written declaration that no inability exists, the Supreme Court shall meet within forty-eight hours to decide whether such be the case and such decision shall be final. Upon a decision that no inability exists, the Governor shall resume the powers and duties of the office.

(e) Whenever there is a vacancy in both the office of Governor and Lieutenant Governor, the General Assembly shall convene in joint session forty-eight hours after such occurrence and elect a Governor from and of the same political party as the immediately past Governor by a majority vote of each house. If either house of the General Assembly is unable to assemble a quorum of its members because of vacancies in the membership of that house, the General Assembly shall convene not later than forty-eight hours after a sufficient number of the vacancies are filled to provide a quorum of members for that house.

(f) An individual holding one (1) of the following offices shall discharge the powers and duties of the governor if the office of governor and the office of lieutenant governor are both vacant, in the order listed:

(1) The speaker of the house of representatives.

(2) The president pro tempore of the senate, if the office described in subdivision (1) is vacant.

(3) The treasurer of state, if the offices described in subdivisions (1) and (2) are vacant.

(4) The auditor of state, if the offices described in subdivisions (1) through (3) are vacant.

(5) The secretary of state, if the offices described in subdivisions (1) through (4) are vacant.

(6) The state superintendent of public instruction, if the offices described in subdivisions (1) through (5) are vacant.

(g) An individual's authority to discharge the governor's powers and duties under subsection (f) ends when the general assembly fills the office of governor under this section.

Section 11. President of the Senate

Whenever the Lieutenant Governor shall act as Governor, or shall be unable to attend as President of the Senate, the Senate shall elect one of its own members as President for the occasion.

Section 12. Commander-in-Chief

The Governor shall be commander-in-chief of the armed forces, and may call out such forces, to execute the laws, or to suppress insurrection, or to repel invasion.

Section 13. Recommendations

The Governor shall, from time to time, give to the General Assembly information touching the condition of the State, and recommend such measures as he shall judge to be expedient.

Section 14. Action on Bills

(a) Every bill which shall have passed the General Assembly shall be presented to the Governor. The Governor shall have seven days after the day of presentment to act upon such bill as follows:

(1) He may sign it, in which event it shall become a law.

(2) He may veto it:

(A) In the event of a veto while the General Assembly is in session, he shall return such bill, with his objections, within seven days of presentment, to the House in which it originated. If the Governor does not return the bill within seven days of presentment, the bill becomes a law notwithstanding the veto.

(B) If the Governor returns the bill under clause (A), the House in which the bill originated shall enter the Governor's objections at large upon its journals and proceed to reconsider and vote upon whether to approve the bill. The bill must be reconsidered and voted upon within the time set out in clause (C). If, after such reconsideration and vote, a majority of all the members elected to that House shall approve the bill, it shall be sent, with the Governor's objections, to the other House, by which it shall likewise be reconsidered and voted upon, and, if approved by a majority of all the members elected to that House, it shall be a law.

(C) If the Governor returns the bill under clause (A), the General Assembly shall reconsider and vote upon the approval of the bill before the final adjournment of the next regular session of the General Assembly that follows the regular or special session in which the bill was originally passed. If the House in which the bill originated does not approve the bill under clause (B), the other House is not required to reconsider and vote upon the approval of the bill. If, after voting, either House fails to approve the bill within this time, the veto is sustained.

(D) In the event of a veto after final adjournment of a session of the General Assembly, such bill shall be returned by the Governor to the House in which it originated on the first day that the General Assembly is in session after such adjournment, which House shall proceed in the same manner as with a bill vetoed before adjournment. The bill must be reconsidered and voted upon within the time set out in clause (C). If such bill is not so returned, it shall be a law notwithstanding such veto.

(3) He may refuse to sign or veto such bill in which event it shall become a law without his signature on the eighth day after presentment to the Governor.

(b) Every bill presented to the Governor which is signed by him or on which he fails to act within said seven days after presentment shall be filed with the Secretary of State within ten days of presentment. The failure to so file shall not prevent such a bill from becoming a law.

(c) In the event a bill is passed over the Governor's veto, such bill shall be filed with the Secretary of State without further presentment to the Governor, provided that, in the event of such passage over the Governor's veto in the next succeeding General Assembly, the passage shall be deemed to have been the action of the General Assembly which initially passed such bill.

Section 15. Transaction of Business

The Governor shall transact all necessary business with the officers of government, and may require information in writing from the officers of the administrative department, upon any subject relating to the duties of their respective offices.

Section 16. Execution of Laws

The Governor shall take care that the laws are faithfully executed.

Section 17. Reprieves—Commutations--Pardons

The Governor may grant reprieves, commutations, and pardons, after conviction, for all offenses except treason and cases of impeachment, subject to such regulations as may be provided by law. Upon conviction for treason, the Governor may suspend the execution of the sentence, until the case has been reported to the General Assembly, at its next meeting, when the General Assembly shall either grant a pardon, commute the sentence, direct the execution of the sentence, or grant a further reprieve. The Governor may remit fines and forfeitures, under such regulations as may be provided by law; and shall report to the General Assembly, at its next meeting, each case of reprieve, commutation, or pardon granted, and also the names of all persons in whose favor remission of fines and forfeitures were made, and the several amounts remitted; provided, however, the

General Assembly may, by law, constitute a council composed of officers of State, without whose advice and consent the Governor may not grant pardons, in any case, except those left to his sole power by law.

Section 18. Vacancies in Office

When, during a recess of the General Assembly, a vacancy shall happen in any office, the appointment to which is vested in the General Assembly; or when, at any time, a vacancy shall have occurred in any other State office, or in the office of Judge of any Court; the Governor shall fill such vacancy, by appointment, which shall expire, when a successor shall have been elected and qualified.

Section 19 Repealed

Section 20. Meeting Place of General Assembly

Should the seat of government become dangerous from disease or a common enemy, the Governor may convene the General Assembly at any other place.

Section 21. Rights and Duties of Lieutenant Governor

The Lieutenant Governor shall, by virtue of his office, be President of the Senate; have a right, when in committee of the whole, to join in debate, and to vote on all subjects; and, whenever the Senate shall be equally divided, he shall give the casting vote.

Section 22. Compensation of Governor

The Governor shall, at stated times, receive for his services a compensation, which shall neither be increased nor diminished, during the term for which he shall have been elected.

Section 23. Compensation of Lieutenant Governor

The Lieutenant Governor, while he shall act as President of the Senate, shall receive, for his services, the same compensation as the Speaker of the House of Representatives; and any person, acting as Governor, shall receive the compensation attached to the office of Governor.

Section 24. Ineligible for Other Office

Neither the Governor nor Lieutenant Governor shall be eligible to any other office, during the term for which he shall have been elected.

ARTICLE VI: ADMINISTRATIVE

Section 1. State Officers

There shall be elected, by the voters of the state, a Secretary, an Auditor and a Treasurer of State, who shall, severally, hold their offices for four years. They shall perform such duties as may be enjoined by law; and no person shall be eligible to either of said offices, more than eight years in any period of twelve years.

Section 2. County Officers

(a) There shall be elected, in each county by the voters thereof, at the time of holding general elections, a Clerk of the Circuit Court, Auditor, Recorder, Treasurer, Sheriff, Coroner, and Surveyor, who shall, severally, hold their offices for four years.

(b) The General Assembly may provide by law for uniform dates for beginning the terms of the county officials listed in subsection (a). If the General Assembly enacts a law to provide a uniform date for beginning the terms of a county official listed in subsection (a), the General Assembly may provide that the term of each county official initially elected after enactment of the law to provide the uniform date for beginning the terms of the county official is for less than four years in order to establish a uniform schedule of dates for the beginning of terms for the office. However, after the initial election for each office, the term for that office shall be for four years.

(c) No person shall be eligible to the office of Clerk, Auditor, Recorder, Treasurer, Sheriff, or Coroner more than eight years in any period of twelve years.

Section 3. Statutory Officers

Such other county and township officers as may be necessary, shall be elected, or appointed, in such manner as may be prescribed by law.

Section 4. Qualifications of County Officers

No person shall be elected, or appointed, as a county officer, who is not an elector of the county and who has not been an inhabitant of the county one year next preceding his election or appointment.

Section 5. Residence of State Officers

(a) The Governor, and the Secretary, Auditor, and Treasurer of State, shall severally keep the public records, books, and papers, in any manner relating to their respective offices, at the seat of government.

(b) The Governor shall reside at the seat of government.

Section 6. Residence of Other Officers

All county, township, and town officers, shall reside within their respective counties, townships, and towns; and shall keep their respective offices at such places therein, and perform such duties, as may be directed by law.

Section 7. Impeachment of State Officers

All State officers shall, for crime, incapacity, or negligence, be liable to be removed from office, either by impeachment by the House of Representatives, to be tried by the Senate, or by a joint resolution of the General Assembly; two-thirds of the members elected to each branch voting, in either case, therefore.

Section 8. Impeachment of Other Officers

All State, county, township, and town officers, may be impeached, or removed from office, in such manner as may be prescribed by law.

Section 9. Vacancies

Vacancies in county, township, and town offices, shall be filled in such manner as may be prescribed by law.

Section 10. County Boards

The General Assembly may confer upon the boards doing county business in the several counties, powers of a local, administrative character.

Section 11. Repealed

ARTICLE VII: JUDICIAL

Section 1. Judicial Power

The judicial power of the State shall be vested in one Supreme Court, one Court of Appeals, Circuit Courts, and such other courts as the General Assembly may establish.

Section 2. Supreme Court

The Supreme Court shall consist of the Chief Justice of the State and not less than four nor more than eight associate justices; a majority of whom shall form a quorum. The court may appoint such personnel as may be necessary.

Section 3. Chief Justice

The Chief Justice of the State shall be selected by the judicial nominating commission from the members of the Supreme Court and he shall retain that office for a period of five years, subject to reappointment in the same manner, except that a member of the Court may resign the office of Chief Justice without resigning from the Court. During a vacancy in the office of Chief Justice caused by absence, illness, incapacity or resignation all powers and duties of that office shall devolve upon the member of the Supreme Court who is senior in length of service and if equal in length of service the determination shall be by lot until such time as the cause of the vacancy is terminated or the vacancy is filled. The Chief Justice of the State shall appoint such persons as the General Assembly by law may provide for the administration of his office. The Chief Justice shall have prepared and submit to the General Assembly regular reports on the condition of the courts and such other reports as may be requested.

Section 4. Jurisdiction of Supreme Court

The Supreme Court shall have no original jurisdiction except in admission to the practice of law; discipline or disbarment of those admitted; the unauthorized practice of law; discipline, removal and retirement of justices and judges; supervision of the exercise of jurisdiction by the other courts of the State; and issuance of writs necessary or appropriate in aid of its jurisdiction. The Supreme Court shall exercise appellate jurisdiction under such terms and conditions as specified by rules except that appeals from a judgment imposing a sentence of death shall be taken directly to the Supreme Court. The Supreme Court shall have, in all appeals of criminal cases, the power to review all questions of law and to review and revise the sentence imposed.

Section 5. Court of Appeals

The Court of Appeals shall consist of as many geographic districts and sit at such locations as the General Assembly shall determine to be necessary. Each geographic district of the Court shall consist of three judges. The judges of each geographic district shall appoint such personnel as the General Assembly may provide by law.

Section 6. Jurisdiction of Court of Appeals

The Court shall have no original jurisdiction, except that it may be authorized by rules of the Supreme Court to review directly decisions of administrative agencies. In all other cases, it shall exercise appellate jurisdiction under such terms and conditions as the Supreme Court shall specify by rules which shall, however, provide in all cases an absolute right to one appeal and to the extent provided by rule, review and revision of sentences for defendants in all criminal cases.

Section 7. Judicial Circuits

The State shall, from time to time, be divided into judicial circuits; and a Judge for each circuit shall be elected by the voters thereof. He shall reside within the circuit and shall have been duly admitted to practice law by the Supreme Court of Indiana; he shall hold his office for the term of six years, if he so long behaves well.

Section 8. Circuit Courts

The Circuit Courts shall have such civil and criminal jurisdiction as may be prescribed by law.

Section 9. Judicial Nominating Commission

There shall be one judicial nominating commission for the Supreme Court and Court of Appeals. This commission shall, in addition, be the commission on judicial qualifications for the Supreme Court and Court of Appeals.
The judicial nominating commission shall consist of seven members, a majority of whom shall form a quorum, one of whom shall be the Chief Justice of the State or a Justice of the Supreme Court whom he may designate, who shall act as chairman. Those admitted to the practice of law shall elect three of their number to serve as members of said commission. All elections shall be in such manner as the General Assembly may provide. The Governor shall appoint to the commission three citizens, not admitted to the practice of law. The terms of office and compensation for members of a judicial nominating commission shall be fixed by the General Assembly. No member of a judicial nominating commission other than the Chief Justice or his designee shall hold any other salaried public office. No member shall hold an office in a political party or organization. No member of the judicial nominating commission shall be eligible for appointment to a judicial office so long as he is a member of the commission and for a period of three years thereafter.

Section 10. Selection of Justices of the Supreme Court and Judges of the Court of Appeals

A vacancy in a judicial office in the Supreme Court or Court of Appeals shall be filled by the Governor, without regard to political affiliation, from a list of three nominees presented to him by the judicial nominating commission. If the Governor shall fail to make an appointment from the list within sixty days from the day it is presented to him, the appointment shall be made by the Chief Justice or the acting Chief Justice from the same list.
To be eligible for nomination as a justice of the Supreme Court or Judge of the Court of Appeals, a person must be domiciled within the geographic district, a citizen of the United States, admitted to the practice of law in the courts of the State for a period of not less than ten (10) years or must have served as a judge of a circuit, superior or criminal court of the State of Indiana for a period of not less than five (5) years.

Section 11. Tenure of Justices of Supreme Court and Judges of the Court of Appeals

A justice of the Supreme Court or Judge of the Court of Appeals shall serve until the next general election following the expiration of two years from the date of appointment, and subject to approval or rejection by the electorate, shall continue to serve for terms of ten years, so long as he retains his office. In the case of a justice of the Supreme Court, the electorate of the entire state shall vote on the question of approval or rejection. In the case of judges of the Court of Appeals the electorate of the geographic district in which he serves shall vote on the question of approval or rejection.

Every such justice and judge shall retire at the age specified by statute in effect at the commencement of his current term. Every such justice or judge is disqualified from acting as a judicial officer, without loss of salary, while there is pending:

(1) an indictment or information charging him in any court in the United States with a crime punishable as a felony under the laws of Indiana or the United States, or:

(2) a recommendation to the Supreme Court by the commission on judicial qualifications for his removal or retirement.

On recommendation of the commission on judicial qualifications or on its own motion, the Supreme Court may suspend such justice or judge from office without salary when in any court in the United States he pleads guilty or no contest or is found guilty of a crime punishable as a felony under the laws of Indiana or the United States, or of any other crime that involves moral turpitude under that law. If his conviction is reversed, suspension terminates and he shall be paid his salary for the period of suspension. If he is suspended and his conviction becomes final the Supreme Court shall remove him from office.
On recommendation of the commission on judicial qualifications the Supreme Court may:

(1) retire such justice or judge for disability that seriously interferes with the performance of his duties and is or is likely to become permanent, and:

(2) censure or remove such justice or judge, for action occurring not more than six years prior to the commencement of his current term, when such action constitutes willful misconduct in office, willful and persistent failure to perform his duties, habitual intemperance, or conduct prejudicial to the administration of justice that brings the judicial office into disrepute.
A justice or judge so retired by the Supreme Court shall be considered to have retired voluntarily. A justice or judge so removed by the Supreme Court is ineligible for judicial office and pending further order of the Court he is suspended from practicing law in this State.

Upon receipt by the Supreme Court of any such recommendation, the Court shall hold a hearing, at which such justice or judge is entitled to be present, and make such determinations as shall be required. No justice shall participate in the determination of such hearing when it concerns himself. The Supreme Court shall make rules implementing this section and provide for convening of hearings. Hearings and proceedings shall be public upon request of the justice or judge whom it concerns.

No such justice or judge shall, during his term of office, engage in the practice of law, run for elective office other than a judicial office, directly or indirectly make any contribution to, or hold any office in, a political party or organization or take part in any political campaign.

Section 12. Substitution of Judges

The General Assembly may provide, by law, that the Judge of one circuit may hold the Courts of another circuit, in cases of necessity or convenience; and in case of temporary inability of any Judge, from sickness or other cause, to hold the Courts in his circuit, provision may be made, by law, for holding such courts.

Section 13. Removal of Circuit Court Judges and Prosecuting Attorneys

Any Judge of the Circuit Court or Prosecuting Attorney, who shall have been convicted of corruption or other high crime, may, on information in the name of the State, be removed from office by the Supreme Court, or in such other manner as may be prescribed by law.

Section 14. Repealed

Section 15. No Limitation on Term of Office

The provisions of Article 15, Section 2, prohibiting terms of office longer than four years, shall not apply to justices and judges.

Section 16. Prosecuting Attorneys

There shall be elected in each judicial circuit by the voters thereof a prosecuting attorney, who shall have been admitted to the practice of law in this State before his election, who shall hold his office for four years, and whose term of office shall begin on the first day of January next succeeding his election. The election of prosecuting attorneys under this section shall be held at the time of holding the general election in the year 1974 and each four years thereafter.

Section 17. Grand Jury

The General Assembly may modify, or abolish, the grand jury system.

Section 18. Criminal Prosecutions

All criminal prosecutions shall be carried on in the name, and by the authority of the state; and the style of all process shall be: "The State of Indiana."

Section 19. Pay

The Justices of Supreme Court and Judges of the Court of Appeals and of the Circuit Courts shall at stated times receive a compensation which shall not be diminished during their continuance in office.

Section 20. Repealed

Section 21. Repealed

ARTICLE VIII: EDUCATION

Section 1. Common School System

Knowledge and learning, general diffused throughout a community, being essential to the preservation of a free government; it should be the duty of the General Assembly to encourage, by all suitable means, moral, intellectual scientific, and agricultural improvement; and provide, by law, for a general and uniform system of Common Schools, wherein tuition shall without charge, and equally open to all.

Section 2. Common School Fund

The Common School fund shall consist of the Congressional Township fund, and the lands belonging thereto;

The Surplus Revenue fund;
The Saline fund and the lands belonging thereto;

The Bank Tax fund, and the fund arising from the one hundred and fourteenth section of the charter of the State Bank of Indiana;

The fund to be derived from the sale of County Seminaries, and the moneys and property heretofore held for such Seminaries; from the fines assessed for breaches of the penal laws of the State; and from all forfeitures which may accrue;

All lands and other estate which shall escheat to the State, for want of heirs or kindred entitled to the inheritance;

All lands that have been, or may hereafter be, granted to the State, where no special purpose is expressed in the grant, and the proceeds of the sales thereof; including the proceeds of the sales of the Swamp Lands, granted to the State of Indiana by the act of Congress of the twenty eighth of September, eighteen hundred and fifty, after deducting the expense of selecting and draining the same;

Taxes on the property of corporations, that may be assessed by the General Assembly for common school purposes.

Section 3. Principal and Income

The principal of the Common School fund shall remain a perpetual fund, which may be increased, but shall never be diminished; and the income thereof shall be inviolably appropriated to the support of Common Schools, and to no other purpose whatever.[

Section 4. Investment and Distribution

The General Assembly shall invest, in some safe and profitable manner, all such portions of the Common School fund, as have not heretofore been entrusted to the several counties and shall make provision, by law, for the distribution, among the several counties, of the interest thereof.

Section 5. Reinvestment

If any county shall fail to demand its proportion of such interest, for Common School purposes, the same shall be reinvested, for the benefit of such county.

Section 6. Liability of Counties

The several counties shall be held liable for the preservation of so much of the said fund as may be entrusted to them, and for the payment of the annual interest thereon.

Section 7. Trust Funds

All trust funds, held by the State, shall remain inviolate, and be faithfully and exclusively applied to the purposes for which the trust was created.

Section 9. Superintendent of Public Instruction

There shall be a State Superintendent of Public Instruction, whose method of selection, tenure, duties and compensation shall be prescribed by law.

ARTICLE IX: STATE INSTITUTIONS

Section 1. Deaf, Mute, Blind, and the Insane

It shall be the duty of the General Assembly to provide, by law, for the support of institutions for the education of the deaf, the mute, and the blind; and, for the treatment of the insane.

Section 2. Juvenile Offenders

The General Assembly shall provide institutions for the correction and reformation of juvenile offenders.

Section 3. County Farms

The counties may provide farms, as an asylum for those persons who, by reason of age, infirmity, or other misfortune, have claims upon the sympathies and aid of society.

ARTICLE X: FINANCE

Section 1. Assessment and Taxation

(a) Subject to this section, the General Assembly shall provide, by law, for a uniform and equal rate of property assessment and taxation and shall prescribe regulations to secure a just valuation for taxation of all property, both real and personal.

(b) A provision of this section permitting the General Assembly to exempt property from taxation also permits the General Assembly to exercise its legislative power to enact property tax deductions and credits for the property. The General Assembly may impose reasonable filing requirements for an exemption, deduction, or credit.

(c) The General Assembly may exempt from property taxation any property in any of the following classes:

(1) Property being used for municipal, educational, literary, scientific, religious, or charitable purposes.

(2) Tangible personal property other than property being held as an investment.

(3) Intangible personal property.

(4) Tangible property, including curtilage, used as a principal place of residence by an:

(A) owner of the property;

(B) individual who is buying the tangible property under a contract; or

(C) individual who has a beneficial interest in the owner of the tangible property.

(d) The General Assembly may exempt any motor vehicles, mobile homes (not otherwise exempt under this section), airplanes, boats, trailers, or similar property, provided that an excise tax in lieu of the property tax is substituted therefore.

(e) This subsection applies to property taxes first due and payable in 2012 and thereafter. The following definitions apply to subsection (f) This subsection applies to property taxes first due and payable in 2012 and thereafter. The General Assembly shall, by law, limit a taxpayer's property tax liability as follows:

(1) "Other residential property" means tangible property (other than tangible property described in subsection (c)(4)) that is used for residential purposes.
(2) "Agricultural land" means land devoted to agricultural use.
(3) "Other real property" means real property that is not tangible property described in subsection (c)(4), is not other residential property, and is not agricultural land.

(f) This subsection applies to property taxes first due and payable in 2012 and thereafter. The General Assembly shall, by law, limit a taxpayer's property tax liability as follows:

(1) A taxpayer's property tax liability on tangible property described in subsection (c)(4) may not exceed one percent (1%) of the gross assessed value of the property that is the basis for the determination of property taxes.
(2) A taxpayer's property tax liability on other residential property may not exceed two percent (2%) of the gross assessed value of the property that is the basis for the determination of property taxes.
(3) A taxpayer's property tax liability on agricultural land may not exceed two percent (2%) of the gross assessed value of the land that is the basis for the determination of property taxes.
(4) A taxpayer's property tax liability on other real property may not exceed three percent (3%) of the gross assessed value of the property that is the basis for the determination of property taxes.

(5) A taxpayer's property tax liability on personal property (other than personal property that is tangible property described in subsection (c)(4) or personal property that is other residential property) within a particular taxing district may not exceed three percent (3%) of the gross assessed value of the taxpayer's personal property that is the basis for the determination of property taxes within the taxing district.

(g) This subsection applies to property taxes first due and payable in 2012 and thereafter. Property taxes imposed after being approved by the voters in a referendum shall not be considered for purposes of calculating the limits to property tax liability under subsection (f). (h) As used in this subsection, "eligible county" means only a county for which the General Assembly determines in 2008 that limits to property tax liability as described in subsection (f) are expected to reduce in 2010 the aggregate property tax revenue that would otherwise be collected by all units of local government and school corporations in the county by at least twenty percent (20%). The General Assembly may, by law, provide that property taxes imposed in an eligible county to pay debt service or make lease payments for bonds or leases issued or entered into before July 1, 2008, shall not be considered for purposes of calculating the limits to property tax liability under subsection (f). Such a law may not apply after December 31, 2019.

Section 2. Disposition of Revenue

All the revenues derived from the sale of any of the public works belonging to the State, and from the net annual income thereof, and any surplus that may, at any time, remain in the Treasury, derived from taxation for general State purposes, after the payment of the ordinary expenses of the government, and of the interest on bonds of the State, other than Bank bonds; shall be annually applied, under the direction of the General Assembly, to the payment of the principal of the Public Debt.

Section 3. Appropriations

No money shall be drawn from the Treasury, but in pursuance of appropriations made by law.

Section 4. Publication of Statement

An accurate statement of the receipts and expenditures of the public money, shall be published with the laws of each regular session of the General Assembly.

Section 5. State Debt

No law shall authorize any debt to be contracted, on behalf of the State, except in the following cases: to meet casual deficits in the revenue; to pay the interest on the State Debt; to repel invasion, suppress insurrection, or, if hostilities be threatened, provide for the public defense.

Section 6. Counties

No county shall subscribe for stock in any incorporated company, unless the same be paid for at the time of such subscription; nor shall any county loan its credit to any incorporated company, nor borrow money for the purpose of taking stock in any such company; nor shall the General Assembly ever, on behalf of the State, assume the debts of any county, city, town, or township; nor of any corporation whatever.

Section 7. Wabash and Erie Canal

No law or resolution shall ever be passed by the General Assembly of the State of Indiana, that shall recognize any liability of this State to pay or redeem any certificate of stock issued in pursuance of an act entitled "An Act to provide for the funded debt of the State of Indiana, and for the completion of the Wabash and Erie Canal to Evansville," passed January 19th, 1846; and an act supplemental to said act, passed January 29th,

1847, which, by the provisions of the said acts, or either of them, shall be payable exclusively from the proceeds of the canal lands, and the tolls and revenues of the canal, in said acts mentioned, and no such certificates or stocks shall ever be paid by this State.

Section 8. Income Tax

The general assembly may levy and collect a tax upon income, from whatever source derived, at such rates, in such manner, and with such exemptions as may be prescribed by law.

ARTICLE XI: CORPORATIONS

Section 1. Banks

The General Assembly shall not have power to establish, or incorporate, any bank or banking company, or moneyed institution, for the purpose of issuing bills of credit, or bills payable to order or bearer, except under the conditions prescribed in this Constitution.

Section 2. Laws

No banks shall be established otherwise than under a general banking law, except as provided in the fourth section of this article.

Section 3. Money

If the General Assembly shall enact a general banking law, such law shall provide for the registry and countersigning, by an officer of State, of all paper credit designed to be circulated as money; and ample collateral security, readily convertible into specie, for the redemption of the same in gold or silver, shall be required; which collateral security shall be under the control of the proper officer or officers of State.

Section 4. Branches

The General Assembly may also charter a bank with branches, without collateral security as required in the preceding section.

Section 5. Responsibility of Branches

If the General Assembly shall establish a bank with branches, the branches shall be mutually responsible for each other's liabilities upon all paper credit issued as money.

Section 6 Repealed

Section 7. Redemption

All bills or notes issued as money shall be, at all times, redeemable in gold or silver; and no law shall be passed, sanctioning, directly or indirectly, the suspension, by any bank or banking company of specie payments.

Section 8. Preference

Holders of bank notes shall be entitled, in case of insolvency, to preference of payment over all other creditors.

Section 9. Interest

No bank shall receive, directly or indirectly, a greater rate of interest than shall be allowed, by law, to individuals loaning money.

Section 10. Repealed

Section 11. Trust Funds

The General Assembly is not prohibited from investing the Trust Funds in a bank with branches; but in case of such investment, the safety of the same shall be guaranteed by unquestionable security.

Section 12. State as Stockholder

The State shall not be a stockholder in any bank; nor shall the credit of the State ever be given, or loaned, in aid of any person, association or corporation; nor shall the State become a stockholder in any corporation or association. However, the General Assembly may by law, with limitations and regulations, provide that prohibitions in this section do not apply to a public employee retirement fund.

Section 13. Other Corporations Formation

Corporations, other than banking, shall not be created by special act, but may be formed under general laws.

Section 14. Liability

Dues from corporations shall be secured by such individual liability of the stockholders, or other means, as may be prescribed by law.

ARTICLE XII: MILITIA

Section 1. Composition

A militia shall be provided and shall consist of all persons over the age of seventeen (17) years, except those persons who may be exempted by the laws of the United States or of this state. The militia may be divided into active and inactive classes and consist of such military organizations as may be provided by law.

Section 2. Commander-in-Chief

The Governor is Commander-in-Chief of the militia and other military forces of this state.

Section 3. Adjutant General

There shall be an Adjutant General, who shall be appointed by the Governor.

Section 4. Conscientious Objectors

No person, conscientiously opposed to bearing arms, shall be compelled to do so in the militia.

Section 5. Repealed

Section 6. Repealed

ARTICLE XIII: POLITICAL AND MUNICIPAL CORPORATIONS

Section 1. Debt Limitations

No political or municipal corporation in this State shall ever become indebted, in any manner or for any purpose, to an amount, in the aggregate, exceeding two per centum on the value of the taxable property within such corporation, to be ascertained by the last assessment for State and county taxes, previous to the incurring of such indebtedness; and all bonds or obligations, in excess of such amount, given by such corporations, shall be void: Provided, That in time of war, foreign invasion, or other great public calamity, on petition of a majority of the property owners in number and value, within the limits of such corporation, the public authorities in their discretion, may incur obligation necessary for the public protection and defense to such amount as may be requested in such petition.

ARTICLE XIV: BOUNDARIES

Section 1. State

In order that the boundaries of the State may be known and established, it is hereby ordained and declared, that the State of Indiana is bounded, on the East, by the meridian line, which forms the western boundary of the State of Ohio; on the South, by the Ohio river, from the mouth of the Great Miami river to the mouth of the Wabash river; on the West, by a line drawn along the middle of the Wabash river, from its mouth to a point where a due north line, drawn from the town of Vincennes, would last touch the northwestern shore of said Wabash river; and, thence, by a due north line, until the same shall intersect an east and west line, drawn through a point ten miles north of the southern extreme of Lake Michigan; on the North, by said east and west line, until the same shall intersect the first mentioned meridian line, which forms the western boundary of the State of Ohio.

Section 2. Jurisdiction and Sovereignty

The State of Indiana shall possess jurisdiction and sovereignty co-extensive with the boundaries declared in the preceding section; and shall have concurrent jurisdiction, in civil and criminal cases, with the State of Kentucky on the Ohio river, and with the State of Illinois on the Wabash river. so far as said rivers form the common boundary between this State and said States respectively.

ARTICLE XV: MISCELLANEOUS

Section 1. Selection of Officers

All officers, whose appointment is not otherwise provided for in this Constitution, shall be chosen in such manner as now is, or hereafter may be, prescribed by law.

Section 2. Duration of Office

When the duration of any office is not provided for by this Constitution, it may be declared by law; and, if not so declared, such office shall be held during the pleasure of the authority making the appointment. But the General Assembly shall not create any office, the tenure of which shall be longer than four years.

Section 3. Extension of Office

Whenever it is provided in this Constitution, or in any law which may be hereafter passed, that any officer, other than a member of the General Assembly, shall hold his office for any given term, the same shall be construed to mean, that such officer shall hold his office for such term, and until his successor shall have been elected and qualified.

Section 4. Oath

Every person elected or appointed to any office under this Constitution, shall, before entering on the duties thereof, take an oath or affirmation, to support the Constitution of this State, and of the United States, and also an oath of office.

Section 5. State Seal

There shall be a Seal of State, kept by the Governor for official purposes, which shall be called the Seal of the State of Indiana.

Section 6. Commissions

All commissions shall issue in the name of the State, shall be signed by the Governor, sealed with the State Seal, and attested by the Secretary of State.

Section 7. County Areas

No county shall be reduced to an area less than four hundred square miles; nor shall any county, under that area, be further reduced.

Section 8. Repealed

Section 9. State Grounds
The following grounds owned by the State in Indianapolis, namely: the State House Square, the Governor's Circle, and so much of out-lot numbered one hundred and forty-seven, as lies north of the arm of the Central Canal, shall not be sold or leased.

Section 10. Tippecanoe Battle Ground

It shall be the duty of the General Assembly, to provide for the permanent enclosure and preservation of the Tippecanoe Battle Ground.

ARTICLE XVI: AMENDMENTS

Section 1. Amendments

(a) An amendment to this Constitution may be proposed in either branch of the General Assembly. If the amendment is agreed to by a majority of the members elected to each of the two houses, the proposed amendment shall, with the yeas and nays thereon, be entered on their journals, and referred to the General Assembly to be chosen at the next general election.

(b) If, in the General Assembly so next chosen, the proposed amendment is agreed to by a majority of all the members elected to each House, then the General Assembly shall submit the amendment to the electors of the State at the next general election.

(c) If a majority of the electors voting on the amendment ratify the amendment, the amendment becomes a part of this Constitution.

Section 2. Submission

If two or more amendments shall be submitted at the same time, they shall be submitted in such manner that the electors shall vote for or against each of such amendments separately.

SCHEDULE

Whenever a portion of the citizens of the counties of Perry and Spencer, shall deem it expedient to form, of the contiguous territory of said counties, a new County, it shall be the duty of those interested in the organization of such new county, to lay off the same, by proper metes and bounds, of equal portions as nearly as practicable, not to exceed one-third of the territory of each of said counties. The proposal to create such new county shall be submitted to the voters of said counties, at a general election, in such manner as shall be prescribed by law. And if a majority of all the votes given at said election, shall be in favor of the organization of said new county, it shall be the duty of the General Assembly to organize the same, out of the territory thus designated.

The General Assembly may alter or amend the charter of Clarksville, and make such regulations as may be necessary for carrying into effect the objects contemplated in granting the same; and the funds belonging to said town shall be applied, according to the intention of the grantor.